1

Orgy of Words
Salacious Short Stories in Poetic Prose

by Branch Isole

Orgy of Words
Salacious Short Stories in Poetic Prose
by Branch Isole

Library of Congress Control Number:
2010922677
ISBN 978-0982658529
eBook ISBN 978-0983574569

MANA'O PUBLISHING

Home of the VOYEURISTIC POET

Manao Publishing
Hampton, VA 23666

Order copies of this book at
www.branchisole.com
www.manaopublishing.com

As a poet and storyteller I observe and comment on the motivations of our world both clothed and bare. Writing of adult issues and emotions often experienced but not always voiced, my style and presentation casts reflective identity against a backdrop of personal responsibility choice or avoidance. This is 'Voyeurism Poetry'.

Orgy of Words contains adult themes and language, all of which are erotic or sexual in nature and presentation. Orgy of Words is intended for mature audiences.

Voyeurism Poetry ~ looking out, seeing in ™

"Many write of things
known or experienced,
I comment on those seen and heard."

"My mind is filled with an orgy of words
each awaiting its appointed time and turn
its singular soliloquized and opportune moment
to travel its downward path

Then to slip
explode
or burst forth
from my pen"

Contents

Introduction

Sexuality.
It is this single common denominator among all
species within the animal kingdom, which
envelopes the power and desire to drive both
dominance and destruction.

As with the dichotomy of life and death,
mankind's sexual expression rides on the
crosscurrents of sin and salvation.

Without it we fail to exist. With it our actions
are influenced, our motives suspect and our
greatness questioned.

How can the discharge of an amalgamation of
feelings contain such pent up emotional energy?
Only its creator understands the simple
complexity of its dual purpose and roles.

Sexual Tension;
Religion uses it for control.
Industry uses it for profit.
The poet uses it for expression.

Branch Isole
the Voyeuristic Poet

"I address myself
only to those persons
capable of hearing me"

~ Donatien Alphonse François de Sade,
the Marquis de Sade

Affair

Be it media mogul celebrities
who met on 'the set'
we're told via tabloid tales
Or a husband, wife duo
living next door
Is the 'love' expressed
any less real
Is the lust experienced
filled with any less 'feel'
for them?

Of hurt and pain
will the onslaught
being cached in clandestine reserve
soon to be known
prove any less damaging
for partners and children
left at home,
who wait patiently
to be touched
within the marrow of bone
by revelations of infidelity
drawing near,
welling up,
reservoirs of torrent tears
which across entire families
will flow like rain

Of promises made
vows now forsaken
will these lovers in their dream state
be awakened
by the sweep of reality's nightmare unleashed
by legality's sharks
who shear and fleece
for the joy, for the bucks
protracted and taken
in reveled exchange
of each hidden copulation tryst
disguised as love-making

Digging deeper the hole of self
indulgence, disgust
for violations, deceit,
abuse of one's trust
Ages old axiom
repetitively ignored
when beyond arm's length
we dare to explore
And so once more
we come to know
inevitably, we reap that which we sow

Anticipation

My heart stops each time the phone rings.
The catch in my breathing chokes
as I wait to hear your name identified out loud.

We've spoken and spat of our secret.
Proclaiming acknowledgement
of our lust's initial shared understanding.
Me insistent. You half-hearted.

Your insecure threats hang over me.
Their preponderance
as if a guillotine blade
poised to be loosed,
waiting to cleave the momentary pause
between bouts of anticipation of you
and the guilt of a characterless vow
made to my spouse.

Revelation doggedly shadows
our movements in public.
Darting clandestinely, wondering,
if the entity which is us
will accidentally be exposed
by friends or acquaintances
from my other life.

You torture by innuendo
when we are apart
and tantalize with orifices
as we copulate.

You don't own me,
I proceed willingly
into the slavery
of your sexual proclivities

and yet

aware we have no future
our abuses continue.

Bachelor

It started with Nancy
'Golden Shower' girl was she
liked to travel and cruise
the open high seas

Along came Janice
who liked being on top
that sexy girl never wanted to stop
Each time we hit
her tender 'G Spot'
she would go into
orgasmic shock

Balancing her with Carol
was quite a feat
insuring the two of them
never would meet
Carol was
another man's whore
she liked me to use
her back door

Then there was my brother's
mother in law
We met at a motel
in Stanislaus

Did Julie's boss,
her best friend from work
Said she wanted my 'lollipop'
to lick and to slurp

Judy Judy Judy
would do
any and everything
for a good screw

Along came Jill
from up the hill
Like to give hummers
just for the thrill

Reminds me of Mike
yes, that was her name
Did it all with a smile
and never was shamed

Mercy came
came on like a flood
She'd do it anywhere
in water or mud

Peggy and Robbie
wouldn't give head
for them sex was always
'Missionary' in bed

Met sweet Marla
Forty-Two double D
Those at least
I wanted to see
To touch
or suckle
actually, hopefully both
Then squirt on her face
and down her throat

Kathy said she wanted
to start each day
with a little or a lot
of heated foreplay

Carla took me
in her hand
and stroked my ever
enlarging male gland
Licked the tip
to get the last drop,
then never ever
wanted to stop
Got on all fours
and looked back with a smile
saying "Come inside big boy
and stay for a while"

Lisa like a rabbit
ready to go
but she never ever
learned how to blow

Noel was running
from her past
Looking for her future's next
to be her last
Shyly got naked
wouldn't be touched
Then I realized
this girl was touched

Lawyer Linda liked to play golf
Came on vacation to play a round
and have some
much needed fun
Took out a club
and her golf ben-wa balls
Hid each and said
"there's still room for you"
Then invited me
to sink a hole in one

Kim never teed a golf ball up
but sure like to do it
on the sixteenth green
right next to the cup

I'd like to take a moment
to thank each of you
And although there have been
more than a few
Most names I've forgotten
having no figment to see
And surely for them
I'm not even a synapse memory
For each of you named
herein today
I'd like you to know
You made me a better person
man
lover,
and you each
helped me grow

So whoever I am
at this point in life
Free from struggle
Free from strife
All failures were mine
and I know through and through
all my success
is in part due to you

Barbie

Sweeping, swirling,
gliding on the wing
Thoughts of you
allow my heart to sing
of ages past
present days
futures unknown
Once again, forever alone

One note at a time
struggling to find
just the right
conjunctive rhyme
Blended slowly
from bass and treble
Crescendo building
You,
an unruly rebel

A hungered groupie
caught naked on tour
Enjoying self-indulgence
just once more
Reaching the door
and playing the whore
White knight slaying all
who might steal your amour

Perfection please;
Scalpel
piece by piece,
trim, nip and tuck
Silicone
Cellulite
Collagen
when is it ever enough?
Once, no twice, no wait
yet thrice,
then four,
then…
even more

The house, Picket fence
The cat and the dog
A self-centered mist
Swallowing all who venture
To peer through its fog

Of thought of word of deed
where to look
To find a seed,
one to fulfill
that burning need,
a need of something
greater than greed

Poor and alone
again this to know,
Your thought,
it was always
win
place
or show
Now, where to turn
which way to go?
Where's the shining man
come to claim his own?

What were your dreams
and where did they lead?
Are you still dreaming today
or did they each slip
slowly away?

What does it take
for you to see
Nothing more than you
and your spirit
for me.

Barfly Becky

She flutters,
bar stool to stool
Imbibing, becoming
a drunkard's fool

Believing herself a butterfly
of establishment's seductive genre
Insecurities pitted deep within
keep her cold as tundra

She's every girl's girlfriend
but a real man hater
the truth be told
Yet her obsessive compulsion
for daddy's love later
requires she never
home alone goes

Sacrificially to each
she offers herself up
Talking constantly
running her mouth
Preparing her head
to go slowly south

The only murmuring
these men want to hear
from her incessant pleas to please,
is soft humming
of pursed lips
while down on her knees

She calls herself Lil
the computer techie
but everyone knows her
as Barfly Becky

Beast With Two Backs

The beast with two backs
came to my room last night

Unable to turn
from its mesmerizing sight
I watched it,
with frightful delight

Contorted
Confused
its fluids ran
splattered
and oozed

Over the sheets
onto the bed

Bathing completely
its four heads

Oh how I dreamed
wished and prayed

I too might be
swept away

To be one with its growl
howl and screams
Totally immersed
in its heated extremes

Both drawn to
and disgusted
by its gleaming skin
wondering,
should I join in?

Watching the performance
salivating on the show
a wink and a nod
to let me know
Then asking,
how far I'd like to go?

"Come"
the smiling beast said
"Come"
get on the bed
"Come"
let me have you too
"Come"
I'll consume all of you

I stood,
frozen in time
stepping forward
only in my mind

I sat,
fantasy dissolved
from the room
I wanted to crawl

"Wait,"
said the beast
"before you go
Answer me this
for I want to know"

"Shall we return
tomorrow night?
Or have you seen enough
of this carnal sight?"

Walking away
the scene continued to play
over and over
in my head,
the beast with two backs
wrestling on the bed

Wishing I had
afraid that I might
have become part
of that covetous sight

Blanca

Enlightenment came
as to the power of
'free sample' marketing
the first time
he was with Blanca

Working professionals
at the 'Four Roses' in old Juarez
he'd heard the rumors, tales
of its ladies and girls
satisfyingly giving head

Having passed inspection
for drips or sores
She took his hand
walking beyond the bedroom door
but before negotiations
for services began
she was on her knees
rubbing, licking
his prick to tease

Nibbling oh so lightly
Winking oh so slightly
balls in one palm cupped
his cock began to respond
becoming erect
gently, swiftly
she zipped him back up

He standing, staring
speechless
perplexed
She smiling, with pursed lips
negligee open revealing bare breasts

For his enjoyment
her talents would prove
so much more than ample
as he would no doubt see
from his previously received
'free sample'

Boy Meats Girl

Hurt me
Restrain me
Stomp me
with your stiletto heels
Damn, you're sexy
in leather and lace
Besmirched 'pearl necklace'
across your face

Ambivalence never once entered
their bed
their couch
nor kitchen floor
Even with his stake in her mouth
Her back against
the Frigidaire door

Breaking free
from nylon stockings that bind
Hostage now predator
as tables are turned
Revenge and mayhem
on her mind

Our dominance role played to a "T"
it was one hellacious
exciting trip
Reflectively watching
acting free
as both got off, on
the whip, grip

Peeping through the keyhole
mesmerized by your touch
of self
With a smile so coy
eyeing secret toys
waiting on the shelf

Imagining mind's fantasies
playing, played out
in new sex games
of bottom and top
Knowing once the friction starts
it's haltingly hard
for a feigned cuckold assault to stop

Barking out commands
riding deep from behind
Screams declare
one's coming soon
As a howl is loosed
at an exposed pale moon

The force of lustful love
exhausting
screwed and bent
Two together totally spent

Salivating
Dreaming
Scheming
Tongue licking
Major and minor lip kissing

Hungered arousal
re-building

Sex starved lovers
crescendo re-rising

Catch and Release

Angling for position
Trolling in search of 'the spot'
Bait and tackle precise
Castings long
Coming up short

Sideways glance
A smirk, a smile, pouty lips
A wink, a nod, contact recognition

Reeling slowly at first
Don't want to lose this one
The dance begins
Verbal and non, language of the hunt

Bodies, Minds, Emotions in play

For you, it was not
'what would be
in our interest'
For you, it was pride
born of conquest

A solitary ride,
landing me
within your net of confidence
Mounting me
in temporary elevation
portraying me, your prize
of the moment

Filleting me with your steeled rod
continuing to draw me closer,
enduring a false bravado of feigned concern
each time you penetrated deeper
with your blade of self-indulgence

Unblinking
you offed my ocular scales of delusion
I watched your use
spawn abuse
until you were ready to throw me back
into the cesspool
of collective broken hearts,
for another chance to swim upstream
against the raging current
of low self-esteem

Crusader

Secreting away the key
in place a belted strategy
locking, blocking phallic entry
dialing down erotic proclivity

Tampering temptation's stray
whilst he be away
believing her fruit cloistered
until his triumphant return
on some future day

Her impenetrable mound
now bound
this Crusader's plan
Leaving her but to suck and fondle,
by both mouth and hand

Disguised as Friends

We imagined being friends for a lifetime,
and we are
though we haven't seen or spoken in years
Blood-brothers via experiences of elation
and prodigious hardship tears

Secrets only our gang of four knew
or were privy to
Sharing her,
each of us in her comely openings
as the fourth filmed it for posterity
What a cinematic exposé it turned out to be
a docu-drama of high school angst,
I wonder where Charlotte is today

Conflicts arise, disguised
as opportunities to test the mental mettle
of newly held beliefs
Ordained by an awareness of responsibility.
If it were only that simple

The largest question looming Friday nights was
who would get to use the back seat
at the drive-in
I understand yours died of an overdose
and mine lives in the Back Bay area

I never revealed,
I fucked your mother one afternoon
while waiting for you to return
from choir practice
She stared transfixed
at the crucifix
hanging above the headboard
as I banged at her from behind
What was that about?
Perhaps you know

Stolen moments, Shared memories
the bonding mortar of youth
belying a truth
we believed we knew
based on our collective wealth of experience
Chronology fed, yet stilted
by authoritative necessity
As we were let loose to prey upon idolizers

Five years of co-dependence
Laying a foundation
Building a footfall path,
for friends

Disrespect

With augmentation of your breasts
you now have two perfect
spherical orbs
nestled on your rib cage
riding high upon your chest

It doesn't get
any better than this

Beneath a plunging
scoop neck sheath
as thin as a shadow
hidden in view
by a single layer
of lustrous material
Erect nipples stand
as if brushed by a cool breeze
to interrupt and support
faux silk that flows
Simultaneously
hanging and clinging
it glides to and fro

A style designed
for a romantic eve's quest
glides as water lapping gently
against two areola capped
tide riding buoys
on a sea of flesh

When you scrutinize yourself
in front of your baroque framed
full length mirror
prior to stepping out
into the public domain
are you aware of your appearance?

Or is the sensual attire
accenting your longing gaze
mistakenly thrust
out of place?

We query your steely-eyed glare
aimed in our direction
as our sights were drawn to you
true was your perception
Is your presentation of self
intended to compel
awe struck croonery?
Or are we to ignore your presence
leaving you cloistered
in private oblivion
and self-imaged buffoonery?

You can't have it both ways

You glance back
over your shoulder
piercing
with self-absorbed assertions
to determine if we
continue to stare

At the patch of denim
you've chosen to wear
Which you portend to pass off
as a covering for cheeks
exposed explicitly bare

Armed with your look
to entrap
the same one you used
at your approach
Insuring we noticed
the splayed front flap
triangulated between zipper and pockets

Resembling a double knit suit's
wide open lapels
the metal teeth pointing
to your muffled pelt
With so much pubic bone
brazenly exposed
a finger tip's insertion
would have brushed
your swollen clit's dome

Yes, we saw
we're gaping still
Isn't that what you want?
Isn't that why you flaunt?
Why not simply wear a thong
as the streetwalkers do?

Oh, that isn't you?

True,
at least the hooker
has the courtesy
to be real,
getting paid for that
she's compelled to do
What about you?

Do you want us to look
Or not?. . . .Well, do you?
Which will it be?

You can't have it both ways

Hey there little mama
We see you're expecting
Congrats!

How did we know?

Perhaps it was your exposed
expanding womb
Basking prodigiously
out front it protrudes,
nakedly leading your way

An epidermal bow
acting as the plow
cutting through the atmosphere
burrowing through the thoroughfare
Occupying the area
of your impending approach

As effective as a locomotive's
bare cow-catcher
Clearing the way
Announcing your arrival
Heralding your coming

Now don't misjudge
or mistake
We're happy for your current state
and you certainly have that pre-natal glow
but it's a shame
you've chosen to stain
nature's aura
in a blatant disregard
for common decency
to placate your insecure ego

Having the need to proclaim
your motherhood aloud
Is it also necessary to expose it
totally bare
to an otherwise, adoring crowd?

This pregnancy may be your first
but Believe It Or Not, as Ripley would say
You're not the first
to be in 'the way'

Please show your unborn child
some dignity and reserve
by covering, him or her

Ladies, respect yourself!
Don't present us you
as a piece of meat
or an object of temporary
temporal desire,
to be used, abused
then discarded on the heap
of past mistakes'
burning pyre

What you project
is how you're perceived
What you send out
is what we receive

Domestic Diva

While ironing
she prevaricates,
a certain undulation
accompanies each stroke
Her hips a balanced metronome
of to and fro
conjoined in sync
ebb and flow

As if swaying to the harmony
from a far off collection of musical notes
heard solely by her deafened ear

Looking up
from the Van Heusen Oxford
a smile creeps across her lips,
as if in slow motion
like a glacial fissure
before it becomes
a racing gap of separation
in Antarctic's unintended abyss

A million miles from her domestic duty
at the corner of her eye
she catches the staring glimpse
admiring her nakedness

For that is how she does
her household chores,
'au naturel'

Truly, maid to order

Emote Motif

So,
How does it feel
to be nothing more
than an afterthought?
A visual question mark?
What it is like
to be seen
walking behind a woman
who deems herself,
Queen

One who by the surgeon's skills
so brazenly
and overtly endowed
appears to be carrying
below her chin
two inflated udders
from a Guernsey cow

So,
How does it feel
insecure man
in this day and time
Heeling to her self-believed
false regalia
while walking two steps behind?

Our compliments
to her plastic surgeon
yes that's quite a rack
but doesn't all the extra weight
put a strain upon her back?

Is she as insecure today
as in the moments before
her massive physical transformation?
And did it accomplish
all that was meant
for her mind and body relation?

So,
How does it feel
to be the secondary sight
An object of scorn
jealousy and laughter
As you my man trail behind
and skip, merrily after?

Do you purposely stay
at arm's length away
while in her flowing wake?
The one that ebbs
she thinks,
a presence does it make

So,
How does it feel
Avoiding her eyes,
those that dart and stray
While yours remain focused
on the back of her head,
that you might crawl inside
each night,
while being in her bed?

Our compliments
to her plastic surgeon
he accomplished quite a feat,
when was the last time standing erect
she actually saw her feet?

So,
How does it feel
to know she's casting
alternating glances
of seduction and daggers,
at those who stop and stare
Seen and known
by your heart
Surely you're aware?

So,
How does it feel
Do you ever worry
she may curtly mention
she's leaving you for another,
one who adores her more
Dare you tire
of making her
your idol of attention?

So,
Has she grown weary
of never being looked in the eye
As strangers she and you pass by
ask themselves,
then wonder why?

Our compliments
to her plastic surgeon
she obviously wants
the world to stare,
but my friend
the reality is
the world doesn't care

So,
How does it feel
to appear the lackey
porter of her baggage
wherever she does roam

Waiting upon haltered staggering steps
as she slows to survey
all she mentally owns

We strictly ask
from clinical curiosity
How does it feel
to walk daily behind
a man-made mammary monstrosity?

Fantasia

Subject broached,
times over the years
Agreement,
if there was a 'No'
from any one of three
born of fear or hesitancy
progression further
could
should
would
not be

Baring that
allow curiosity
to enthrall the cat

Nerves subsiding
Looks all around
small talk, touches
heat rising
fantasies abound

Tongues, Lips
Shafts, Tips
Thumbs, Fingers
pleasures linger
Him in her
Her in them
Twisting, Twirling
making heads spin

Filling each other up
with his, with her
licentious smiles
salacious purrs
Restrictions abandoned
once and for all
total sharing
caring
having a ball

One and one and one
make three
sated complete, thoroughly
Each one's
forbidden fruit
picked from the tree

Fit To Be Tied

I don't think
I want to be spanked
I'm all grown up now
too big for that
After all, I'm as lean
as old Jack Sprat
and a good sexual whipping
would touch me
to the bone
(and I can only have
that much fun,
away from home)

Please don't hurt me
I can't stand the pain,
No harder still
make my butt burn and sting
with redness
from your crop
from your whip
from your leather baton toy
I need to be punished
I've been such a bad boy

To control me
with your crop
your whip
your big black wooden paddle
would take me back
in my head,
behind those sacred curtains

I'd feel Father Old Leery's
warm nicotine breath
and hear his old brogue prattle,
confusing me
abusing me
accusing me
of being so bad,
so good,
I'd be wishing again
he could, he would,
wait, maybe not
I'm not really sure
I'm not really me
I'm trapped

Oh you,
you've got me so addled

Fornication Under Command of the King

I've heard it said
this word among words
came from Jolly Old England
In a time when one
would ne'er against the King
take a stand

Whether by right
or command
or acquiescence to obey
This word has certainly
found its way
into mainstream's vernacular today

Once a word
of action taken
Now an adverb
for extensive use to be making

Hearing it verbalized
again and again
As often as every
second or third utterance
by some women
and many men

Its impact lost
Its intensity no more
What once was reserved
for seaman and whore

Is now heard constantly,
a conversational part
No longer genitally based
It's now tied to the heart

One more instance
of mass desensitizing
Like disrespect and mayhem
in society rising

Conversationally coupled
with two close cousins
we now also hear
mo' and mo'
Two denigrating monikers
ascribed to women,
the female descriptors
'bitch and ho'

For those who use it
No view of love
or lusting
Peppering their immature oral excursions
Proves their superfluous language disgusting

Games

You,
the self-proclaimed
Master
If they ever ask me
I'll answer,
Bastard

I haven't got time for your games
Not since you left me

You,
labeled them
'the Grand Dame Games'
As you chipped away
piece by piece,
heart
mind
body and soul
You required
a relinquishing of all
to be part of the ball,
Asshole

I haven't got room for your games
Not since you left me

You,
sweet talking
charmer
with deceit filled
quips
and one liners
Passionate Marquis de Sade
complete with chains
and whips,
Prick

I haven't the mood for your games
Not since you left me

You,
two timer
three
four, maybe more
Stringing each along
a bevy of beauties
in your throng,
Son of a Bitch

I haven't the need for your games
Not since you left me

You,
lying there
in your own fluids and waste

How do you feel now?
where is your smile?
your coy sneer?
oh how sad,
I'm glad
your face is smeared,
blood red
from the bullet hole
in your head

I haven't got time for your games
I haven't got room for your games
I haven't the mood for your games
I haven't the need for your games
Not since you left me

goodbye
forever
this time,
Cocksucker

No
no, no
no more of your games,
Now that you've left me

Glass Ceiling

Always fucked over
Never over fucked

Golden Triangle

"While you're down there"
her sultry voice cooed,
an octave above a whisper

Bent on one knee
to lace his shoe
He stopped himself
from rushing his gaze
up to her face

She had closed
the small distance
between them
and was now standing
hands on hips

Slowly raising his eyes
letting the catch in his sigh slip
he scanned her Lycra clad body
wondering if she noticed
the beads of sweat
which had appeared on
his upper lip

Close enough now
for him to spy
a worn frayed spot
slightly above and left of center
on her right thigh

His eyes automatically drawn
to her pubic region
he noticed
small stains of dampness
Was it her workout?
his emotions asked,
or evidence of her vixen vampness

Dazed, his thoughts traveled afar
as he mentally stumbled
over questions his mind
continued to tumble
'How long had it been there?'
'What was its cause?'
'Had I contributed
to its presence?'

Shuffling quickly
through possibilities
donning his mental shelf
"I can only hope"
he told himself

Hearing the cough
coupled with a soft
"Well?"
trailing off
His senses snapped back
to the silky pasture of skin
he knew lay below
that fabric so thin

Stretching across
her golden triangle
hidden, from every stranger
this area of temptation
pleasure and danger
"Well?" she queried easily once more
"yes" he replied with a rakish grin

Heads

Thinking of you
as I sit at the light
A moment's reflection
upon our last night
The signal's top spot
ever so red
remembering longingly
your comfortable bed

The satin sheets
against my back
Your smiling lips
eyeing my lap
The caress of your hands
upon my thigh
Your tongue on my tip
moving me ever so high

A small bead of moisture
upon your brow
Glistening from the window's ray
I see it now
My hands grasp your hair
as if a mane
Your lips and tongue
drive me slowly insane

If this be insanity
let me revel forever
False promise made
"I will leave you never"

Rapid advance
you continue to make
Liquid love
it all do you take

Finishing me now
the end of the race
Not one droplet
do you waste

Smiling shyly
on your back you roll
Once again
in total control
Upon my psyche
you take its toll

Trying to be strong
try as I might
Heads pulse and pound
still wrapped oh so tight,
at the remembrance of your beauty
in the dawn's daybreak light

Hottie

Sizzlin' baby
that's what you are
When my tips rake your skin
sparks fly
heat rises
blood begins to boil

Charged are you,
exuding sultry sensuality
and comely sexiness

Your aura of surrounding femininity
sprayed as if cosmic rays of energy
beguiles every transfixed eye
drawn in your direction

To have those supple lips slightly parted
a flicking tongue
removing the drop of sweetness
produced by the welling anticipation
of your naked touch,
balancing it for the world to see
before tasting and swallowing
this man made nectar

Straddled atop
ears muffed by silky smooth thighs
staring longingly at your bare mound descending
smothering lips with lips
my tongue searches the sides
which lead upward
to your hooded hidden button
the 'key' to your first stage of pleasure

You electrify my being
as we are joined
our puzzle completed
by penetration and reception
Backs arch as souls scream aloud
and we become one
bucking in unison
until flung afar into solitudes of ecstasy
by orgasmic explosions and release

Bodies flameless fire
radiating desire
produces pools of liquid love

Stroking, stoking
the repository of rekindled embers
of our next ablaze position

How Desperate Am I?

He lied to me
in my bed
He lied to me
when I gave him head
He lied to me
before and after
he had all my holes
but at least in front
of all his friends
he grins and calls me
his only 'Ho'

Gone for three months
I thought I knew
but alas, I didn't
he lied to her too
Returned to find
it was her he was doing
and all along
I believed
it was only me
he was screwing

He lied
He cheated
He went behind my back
but right from the start
he was my heart

I soon found out
everyone knew,
everyone of course except me
Even the soap man
can you believe?

It all worked out
as I hoped it would
For a few days after my return
she realized too
she'd been burned
Took her about four seconds
to kick him to the curb
Gosh, she must be
really disturbed

She said it was
honesty and integrity he lacked
Lucky for me, huh
'cuz I got him back

I know my heart
can't be trusted
he'll do it again
even if busted
I know my heart's love
is no more than a sham
but that goes to show,
how truly desperate I am

Imaginary Lover

Standing motionless,
Camouflaged
I disappear into the landscape
Watching you
through the small window
as you glide effortlessly around the room

You dance and you tease
Always trying to please
Your imaginary lover,
Who is he?

Seeing you
before the mirror
Enjoying
the both of you
Devouring
your every move
The two of you
under the harvest moon

You dance and you tease
Always trying to please
Your imaginary lover,
Who is she?

You twist and you twirl
Arms in the air
Hands in your hair
Two shy girls
Seductively bare

You dance and you tease
Always trying to please
Your imaginary lover,
Might we become three?

Soon my love soon
Soon will two be
Harmoniously in tune
Two will become one my love,
Soon

You dance and you tease
Always trying to please
Your imaginary lover,
is it me?

Internal Affair

First we kissed
then we touched
then more
oh so much

The sex was hot
The guilt was not
Thoughts,
of getting caught
for doing things
that we ought not

I believe I was
as nervous as he,
although it was left
for me to lead

I don't know why
or what made me do it
Honestly,
I'm not sure
I'm not a bad person
(*really*)
Nor a sexual predator
(*I don't believe*)

Was it boredom,
insecurity
self-serving desires?
That he was young
and available
or worse,
that he was easy to control
and coerce?

What started out
as a flirting game
between two well-known strangers
turned ugly and soon,
too soon
was fraught with too much danger

Sneaking around
was half the fun,
until my husband discovered
I was fucking his son

Keyholes

Keys of destiny
Keyholes for practitioners
Expression opportunities
in a thirsting and hungry
deceit filled world
designed to repress

free will reigning supreme
for each here bound
triggered to action
without forethought or plan,
a daunting task
accepting responsibility's yolk

we ask questions about coveted things
for which we have the answers
inculcated within our nature and being;
both spirit and cellular

forces of nature
survival of the fittest
winnowing of the weak
truths of self-reliance

As virgins in the exchange
we wonder why
Hardened through experience
we no longer care to ask
We simply respond and rationalize

Kindred

I plagiarize your vulgarity
hoping to titillate young girls
who know no better,
tasting four letter words
repeated to a blush and giggle

Heartfelt swoons
delivered to tickle ears
with nasty little thoughts
hoping to let on
to harden pulsation innuendos,
as legs cross and uncross
exposing thighs
and shaven pubescent vulvae lips

A-line uniforms trim and crisp
addressing each other as 'slut'
Fabricating bawdy Chaucer-esque tales
Whispering sophisticated ribaldry rail
as if twenty-something vamps
thirty-something scamps
forty-something tramps
or middle aged mothers
disguised as MILF's who share martinis
and cabana
boy-toys

In unison they squeal with glee
trollops declared one and all
Sisterhood of vixens lining up
a daisy chain of flesh
matriculating repertoires on display
juicy fetish devoteés

fingers lightly paw scrota orbs
mouths laud salacious words
master's voice does intone
missies vie for mister's bone

Lost in You

Watching you
from up on high
Visualizing you in my mind
watching me
as I enter you

A sprite's smile
crosses your lips
your eyes roll back
under half closed lids

Sensing your sensation
at your urging of "deeper"
my engorged shaft pulsating
from hilt to throbbing tip
Pushes gently
slowly rolling back
major and minor
swollen lips

Sweet fragranced musk
permeates your opening
which closes tight
around my white hot tusk
Grasping and swallowing
from head to base
leaving, not a trace

Coaxing me in fully
you raise your hips up
drawing heels to you
with upturned hands cupped
Forming two triangles
for our support
Readied for riding
this moment's part
of our afternoon's
love sport

A sideway glance
first one,
then the other
Together we stare
at the mirror's imaged pair
One mounted, twirling
swirling
One writhing
a plunging motion
Two bodies in sync
enjoying lust's
homemade potion

We smile to each other
reversed images show
Other worldly
watching two people coupled
Two we don't yet know

Taking your legs
into my hands
Now they rest,
draped over my shoulders
Grasping your hips,
locking them with my wrists

Lifting to impale you
upon a spike
of eruption's flow
Friction sparking
love's amber glow

Faster,
wet heat surging
bodies' lubricants spill over us
with each of your heightened
downward thrusts

Emanating circle of fire
your hard clitoral button
refuses to tire
Partly hooded
Partly exposed
Kissing my thumb
and forefinger
rubbing, pinching
massaging,
as your moanings linger

"Fill me"
you cry out,
"Give me cock
fill me,
my mouth
my ass
my breasts,
I'm your whore
your pussy galore"

"Rub your cock and balls
all over my body
In and out
Up and down
here, there, all around"

"Penetrate me
everywhere
you dare
For I am yours
at this moment,
no matter the cost"

Ecstasy explosion
Mental erosion
Emotional corrosion
In each other
we are lost

Love Hurts

"I love you" he mused
staring hypnotically
as he slid deep, up inside of her

Eagerly he rode
Stroking his hardened cock,
while pinning her down

"you don't" she mockingly replied
"you love that you're fucking me
like all those other guys"

"fuck off" he snapped, pulling out
turning cold, storming from the room

fetally curled on the floor
awaiting rebirth
as the next john's whore

Love Lost

Loving behavior?
few and far between
Holding of hands?
lost esteem
Love light shining
betwixt four eyes?
Give in, Gave up
not worth the time

Love today?
a word bandied about
on movie screens
In real time most likely
domestic screams

Couples sharing
dishonor, distrust
Histories of exes
past personal baggage
Single digit months
evidence of corroding rust

Love today?
Sans depth beyond
fucking, sucking
objects
adjectives
synonyms of sex

An empty emotion
trying to be filled
by 'Benjamin C-Note' power
and anti-depression pills
Love is meant to be
unconditional
Full of forgiveness
and compassion
To share, give and learn from
Not to be used
abused
held hostage,
penalized or rationed

Love is not of the mind
although we like to think it is
Love is not a physical urge
though its pain
can bring even the mighty down

Love is a soul connection
of spiritually charged energy,
to be given freely
received fully
and shared faithfully

Millennium Foreplay Thought Balloon

If I continue to listen
to your inane orated dribble long enough,
Can I still get my cock sucked?

Oedipus Revisited

Discovering you
could be a full time chore
Finding your line
between Madonna and whore
For my fantasies are
oh so pendular
and yet, I find
none regrettable
Although I do struggle
with those
which are Oedipal

Oh So

You don't need more
than a willingness to show
to get those looks
you crave, oh so
Strolling lanes, trails and paths
clothed oh so scantily clad

Coveting desirous eyes
as if eighteen on tour
Peering coyly
over your shoulder behind
Hoping and praying
theirs are on yours

Please,
give us dogs a break
your rolls of fat
are oh so hard to take
Over-flowing waist bands
Bulging thighs
That much exposed cellulose
strains our oh so tired
doggy style eyes

Unless of course
you wish to use
those oh so fat lipped
adipose grooves
To massage and stroke
our oh so enlarged
blood engorged
male organ tubes

I'm sure by now
you're totally aware
our oh so satisfaction is strictly found
in your two easy access orifices
at either end
of all those pounds

For our tab 'A'
now only oh so fits
in your oral or
anal openings
and occasionally
between your teats

Being oh so fat
in such tight fitting clothes
I'm sure you're aware
as everyone knows
the flour legend of how to help
us dogs find slot 'B'

Then again perhaps
we both can agree
our oh so phallic towers
you can enjoy fucking vaginally

One Hand Clapping

Sex alone,
Tentative
Mental fantasies
Bodily response
in sync
perhaps,
maybe,

eventually

Assuming both roles
simultaneously
conversations and thoughts
Finally a rhythm
of hands and genitals

Sustained fever pitch,
mental
psychological
physical
emotionally draining

What started
as a multitude
of extreme efforts
ends quickly,
As if falling from the sky
like a pole-vaulter
having missed the benchmark,
waiting for the sudden impact
of ground,
unfulfilled

Oral Desires

It was a Friday night,
and Gail had endured a long dry spell
without truly being satisfied.
So much so
the foremost thought
in her mind as she drove
was that of "scoring."

She was confident she knew
which establishment in town,
if one could even call it a town,
where her innermost craving and desires,
those that had been gnawing at her all week
could be sated.

As she thought about how long it had been
since she had "had some"
a devilish voice inside her head whispered,
"You deserve it as much
as any of the others girls in the secretarial pool."
Gail then spoke audibly, as if to a confidant
"Isn't Jane, little Miss prim and proper
on the outside
always confiding in me
how she risks her parents finding out
about her weekends?"

Gail then exclaimed indignantly
to the staring eyes in the rear view mirror
"That doesn't stop her!"

Jane had been getting away with it
for months and no one seemed the wiser.
There was an air of innocence about Jane
but underneath it all Gail knew the truth
surrounding 'Miss Goody Two Shoes.'

Sure, most of the girls in her office
were only one or two years
out of high school
and still legally under age.
"Much too young for drinking
and staying out, carousing at night
with the boys in this town"
her father incessantly reminded her.
It was as if his entire mission in life
had become to make sure
Gail remembered that she was still
only eighteen and living "under his roof"
as was his announced and repeated mantra
each time the subject came up.

Gail really didn't care anymore.
She was ready to cut loose a little
and experience new things.
It was time to 'live it up and paint the town red.'
Yes. That was it. Paint the town Red!
Perhaps she would try to hook up
with notorious 'Big Red.'

That would do it.
She would show them once and for all.
Her parents, the girls at work, all of them.
Just this once
Gail would do what Gail wanted to do.

To hell with them
and all their moralizing, she told herself.

Yes, Big Red
that would do it for sure.
One night with Big Red
and she would finally be free.
Free of her parents, free of this town,
free of all the stares and whispers
from the secretarial pool inhabitants.
They all talked of wanting to try it
but Gail told herself
"Enough talk, it's time for action."
Tonight would be the night
she would seek out Big Red
and take him into her mouth.

On her way to the "Stopwatch"
the town's infamous and only late night bar
she decided to make sure
she had everything needed
to fulfill the intimate thoughts
about the evening ahead
which swept through her mind
like cascading falls.

As she stood at the counter
about to pay for the diet cola
and the package of condoms
she had selected
out of the corner of her eye
she caught a glimpse of Big Red.
Her pupils dilated
as she tried to focus without being obvious.

Sure enough
there was Big Red.

Within a few moments
of leaving hand in hand with Big Red
she had made her decision.
"Why wait any longer?"
the voice whispered to her,
"you're here
Big Red is here
its dark
your car is right outside
the time is now."

Getting into her car
she spoke as if to no one.
"You don't know how long
I have waited and dreamed of this moment."

Driving down Main Street
Gail turned left at the end of the block
heading for the river
and General Lee Park
on the edge of town.

Glancing at Big Red in the passenger seat
she whispered to herself
"Gail, this is your chance
don't lose your nerve now."

Arriving at the park
she picked a dark and secluded spot
where she was sure
they would have privacy.

Turning off the car's engine
she sat and stared at Big Red.

As a coy smile crossed her lips,
"No more waiting" she said.
With quick movements by both hands
she had Big Red released and exposed.

Even in the darkness
she could see Big Red
was already stiff and hard.
The moonlight twinkled and
glistening off the magnificent pink color
which stood erect before her.
Almost salivating, her mind raced
with the thoughts of the sweet taste
within her grasp.

She slowly began to feel it with both hands
Holding it firmly with her left
while up and down the side of the shaft
she lightly moved her fingers.

It felt so smooth and slender
she closed her eyes and lazily dreamed
of the moments to come.
Infatuated with thoughts
of sliding its whole stiffness
into her mouth
she resolved to keep it there
until she was done and satisfied,
until she was ready to release it.
She would take it all in,
hard and stiff

keeping it there until it became
soft and sticky.

Gail could feel the heat rising
within her body
she became uncomfortable with her position.
Gail shifted to face the other seat
"Big Red, I hope you enjoy this
as much as I intend too."
With that she slowly brought it to her face
her lips parted,
Gail took a moment to look down and smile.

As her mouth and hands met
she could begin to taste all its sweetness
on the tip of her tongue.
Gently at first, then a bit more aggressively
she twirled and slid her tongue
back and forth against Big Red's sides.
She could feel Big Red on one cheek now
and then the other.

Up and down, back and forth, to and fro,
Big Red was everywhere inside her mouth
she had taken all of it inside.

As she opened her eyes
she stared at the moon
Gail felt as if she were in heaven
right here on earth.
Yes, she had waited,
but it had been worth every agonizing minute.
"Finally" she thought,
I have crossed that line

I have taken Big Red into my mouth
and made it mine.

To her surprise
this had gone on for at least twenty minutes.
"Where had the time gone?" she asked herself.
It seemed as if only moments ago
Big Red was as hard and stiff
as she could have ever hoped or dreamed of
and now,
it was just as she had suspected
soft and sticky
limp to the touch of her tongue.

She truly enjoyed the minutes
that had slipped away
having Big Red a part of her
becoming one with the object of her oral desires
while Big Red was inside of her.

She thought about its initial sweetness
with a hint of almost cinnamon tartness,
now all but dissipated.

Rolling down the window
as she drove from the park,
she spat out the gum
and decided it was time
for some drinking and dancing, at the Stopwatch
with the ladies from the secretarial pool.

Paradise Found

We met at a bar
on the sands of Waikiki
Her last night in town
drinking Mai Tai
and Long Island Ice Tea

She and a friend
decided to shoot the moon
Get loose, get crazy,
they surveyed the room

Our eyes met,
not fatal attraction
but both of us knew
we were up for some action

Small talk
A couple of jokes
One more round
Outside for a toke

Leaving her friend
and my brother behind
We lay on the sand
and started to grind

Her pelvis in motion
legs interlocked
without adieu
I was hard as a rock

Hands massaging
the small of her back
The smell of her skin
her scent on attack

Stopping a moment
figures on the lanai
She let out a laugh
I thought was a cry

She standing over me
us both now erect
she stripped off her clothes
I said, "What the heck"

We ran naked to the water's edge
as her friend and my brother
looked over the rail
of the patio's ledge

She said "come with me baby"
and sprinted aloft
Breasts bouncing,
hair flowing
bronzed skin,
tan lines showing

Hitting cold water
I went flaccid
and soft

Standing in ocean up to her nipples
arms round my neck
lips to mine
She whispered,, "let's keep this simple"
I moaned,
"That's fine"

Hand in hand
we ran up the beach
a secluded and private
spot did we reach

Relaxing supine
night's sand on my spine
both knew we were in
for one hell of a time

Lips to lips
tongue on the tip
Sixty eight plus one
we both started to lick

Nibble the hood
darting below
sweet musk liquid
started to flow
Thumb and finger
both buried deep
sheath of tissue
wet in between

Dreamily wanting
never to stop
Next thing I knew
she was mounted on top

Large firm breasts
cupped in my hands
Hardened engorged member
wrapped tight by her glands

Up
and
down,
she slowly rode
I fought back the urge
to release all my load

As we thrust rapidly
against one another
squatted above me
she impaled herself
like no other

Both adrift
in our lands of nether
final explosion
we came together

Exhausted and spent
we lay entangled
Two lifeless forms,
racked and mangled

Eye to eye
and breath to breath
smiling broadly she said,
"I have a plane to catch".

Red Robin Hood

Little Red Robin
peeking from beneath her hood
Wishes she might
Hopes she could

Wandering Wolf
smiling ear to ear
"Come closer my dear,
You have nothing to fear"

"But you Sir,
dressed in sheep's garb,
you make it difficult
you make it hard"

Flashing dagger sharp teeth
"Be assured
through and through
yes,
it is hard for you"

"Shall I stay the course
on this path?
Or join you Wolf
in blissful gaff?"

"Whatever you want
sweet, sweet Red
I'm counting on you
to use your head"

"I would love to
be with you
to be caressed
and shown
But my father's mother said
'come straight home' "

"No need Red
to listen to Him
to her
or anyone of them
Somehow we'll get through
just me, just you

For as you must
already know
I am of that other world
The one into which
you desire to go
It is my job
my duty
my task,
to do whatever
you might ask

Your desires and wishes and wants
await
There,
beyond yonder gate

Join me Red
Here,
take my arm
Together we'll stroll
no need for alarm
Through this hallowed gate
is your new world
your new life
your new fate

Look up,
down our new stretch of road
Prepare yourself Red
to take on my load

See here from behind us
comes now the fact
the arrival,
the hungered,
the rest of my pack

Know it
Believe it
For now it is true
My world gives you
your covets,
your desires,
all is for you

You asked for a treat
Now run
or lie down
So we may eat

Through and through
what I want
what was planned
all I intended to do,
is simply and totally
devour you"

Red of the Hood
Who wished she might
Who hoped she could

Revolver

Lifting her high above his head
he allowed her cradled thighs
to drape comfortably over his shoulders.
Drawing her closer
with his forearms against the cheeks of her rump
he could smell her muskiness with his nose
and brush his lips against the moistness of her
black silk panties.

Slowly twirling
as if dancing
oblivious to the members of the crowd
who had gathered to leer
he gently gnawed
then more violently tore
against the fabric
until the stretch
of the elastic spaghetti strap piece
gave way under the tensile strength
of his eye tooth.

As his tongue flicked outward
probing the swelled fleshy skin
gently moving back the cutaneous fold
he could feel his balance shift
at the weight of her careening back in ecstasy
while he licked her clitoral button
and penetrated beneath its hood.

Her blog explained how she had always wanted
to go to the moon.
Clutching the baby in her arms
she pulled the trigger.
Shooting him would give her notoriety
and the media coverage needed
to stockpile money for the trip.

Others had wanted,
had threatened to do the same,
some to his face.
She had waited
until his sexual advance pushed her far enough
that there was no turning back.
At point blank range
she fired two shots.
That would show him and the world
how serious she was about making the trip.

She waited for the police
and news camera crews
measuring out in her head
the space suit she would need
for her first EVA walk.

His roommate was glad it had come to this
before it was left to him
or his estranged brother
to be the ones
who put a stop to his lothario behavior.

He stooped,
bending
and then squatted
for a better vantage point.
Reaching down to pick up the coins
which had fallen.
Clustered between the grass and clumps of dirt
he retrieved the first handful
then uncovered mounds of larger denominations
as his mother said he would,
in her related bedtime stories
from behind the bars of her cell
after she had given birth to him in prison.

Cupping her bicep area
as muffled apnea sounds escaped
he diddled his testicles
her naked slumbering body mere inches away.
Returning to bed
anticipating a fellated frolic
she had drifted off
leaving him to touch
his enlarging penile shaft
with thumb and forefinger
while his pinky digit lightly stroked
the outer edge of his anal sphincter.

Right Now

Right Now,
Right at this very moment
Somewhere in the world
Somewhere on the planet
Someone is,
strolling on a country lane
attending to a chronic pain
receiving a traffic ticket
chasing dinner through a thicket
blowing their stuffy nose
tickling a baby's toes
saying, 'I don't know'
refusing to grow
making mad passionate love
in a park
feeding a dove
inventing a new device
cheating on a cheating wife
quarreling and throwing fists
slicing a pair of wrists
someone is buying
someone is selling
someone is yelling
someone is felling
a tree
one is paying a fee
another is breaking a knee
someone is taking a pea
on a fork
having a snort
filing a legal tort
coming into port

building a cardboard fort
making a caustic retort
just about to abort
passing gas as a smelly fart
throwing a steel tipped dart
going on a summer lark
in a play reciting the line
'Hark'
making a large dog bark
standing stark
naked
a child is saying 'I hate you'
a child is saying 'I love you'
a lady has the flu
a man has lost his shoe
a teenager is turning blue
a crying mother says 'I wish I knew'
a boy really is named Sue
(No not really)
but someone somewhere is peeling
someone else is pealing
and a third is pealing out in a car
burning rubber
one is having supper
another lunch
yet another breakfast
and yet another, brunch
a young woman feels all alone
one is on the phone
someone has just sown
a seed
pulled a weed

been in need
tossing feed
wetting a reed
for a wind instrument
having a fit
suckling a teat
tonguing a clit
as a woman asks
'where are all the good men'?
the Marines say
they have 'a few good men'
a prayer ends with amen
somewhere a rooster chases a hen
a man has just broken his pen
a bank is ready to lend
a shirt is on the mend
a woman is having to fend
off an attacker
someone is playing a hunch
an uncle is throwing a punch
an aunt is feeling the crunch
a toothless man is trying to munch
his snack
before he has his heart attack
someone is coming back
someone is leaving
someone is going home
someone is reading a poem
about
Right Now.

Sailor's Garden

From a long line of agrarians
came a seafaring Aquarian
A farmer at heart
Tall ship, his cart

Tiller in hand
sailing land to new land
His life spent at sea
navigating world round
to port after port
and town after town

At each global place
and every new space
in mound upon mound
did he plow new ground

Longing to be used
for temporary gardening
in pockets at sea
his tools had been hardening

Recounting once more
from long ago past
Recalling sea stories
how to make it last

Excavating fresh ground
each deep furrowed new mound
Pale red earth
pink, supple and sweet
waiting to bear fruit
mind and body complete

Working his hoe
day and night
watching and waiting
this new mound now ripe

He said it is here
in this mound I shall stay
for in this rich moisture
I desire to play,
as a bulbous hood
was plied softly away

Remembering lonely nights at sea
when it was hands on the mast
All efforts now languid
not going too fast

From this seaman
came seeds
which he had brought
in his pulsating quiver
full,
bulging
and hot

Using his tool
each portal received
all efforts to please
one final release

Shuddering acceptance
Long furrow lain
Slow strokes back and forth
Sun's trek was now stayed

Sun once more dawning
Sailing visitor did sow
Receiver of life's seed
now gloriously aglow

Using his hoe
in this warmth he did know
the taste of sweet fruit
from one local grove

Awaiting rekindling of his planting desire
stoking flames to recreate intensity's fire
He would once more a furrow plow
filling her ripe and ready bowels
with bursting buds of husbandry
before returning to the sea

Alas however, it was not to be
Watching tearfully
he slipped back to the sea

Her sailing farmer
and his ship so tall
neither to return
until the next fall

Now is the garden
eager and willing
to receive her sailor
for more rapturous tilling
For when he returns
all brush be removed
for where once was
but barren ground,
now a rich and moist
fertile mound
doth abound

Sex Sells

Decked out,
dressed to the nines
Now, no longer confined

In a past perceived
as a living hell
Now to discover
if sex really sells

Time to penetrate
the bond tightly bound
between these three
Time to find out single handedly
where fun and fame and fortune be found

Peahen parading
pretentious prance
Questing a colorful
preening new mate
with whom to dance
Not at heaven's Pearly
but at gold's gilded gates

Head held high
Back is straight
Bust protrudes suggestively
Flag is up
Game of coy is on
Goal to become
a local celebrity

It's about the money,
then the fun
Becoming known
as number one
Learn to put aside
the guilt, the shame
It's all for money's
salacious ride
on the coat-tails of
new found fame

Attention disorder
was her plea
"All attention
must be on me"
Not a true 'gold digger'
as one might say
But the notches on her bed posts
did convey
the fun, fame and fortune
she craved

She Said

"Here comes
the good stuff,"
she said
Almost in a whisper
just loud enough
to hear

Free sample
given and received
Time spent
on her knees
Cool kisses
fresh as a breeze
Oh how that girl
could tease
and please

Fireman's cap
highly exposed
cocked, loaded
ready to explode

Ever so slowly
with her brass ring
Around his maypole shaft
did she sing

Enjoyment from thumbs
fingertips
body parts
She titillated,
even his heart

From head to toe
and back again
she left his heads
in a spin

She was one
who knew her stuff
Never too little
just enough
Almost in a whisper
just loud enough to hear
leaning against him on the bed,
"Here comes the good stuff,"
she said

Sleeping With You

When sleep whispers
and calls to me
I always go willingly
For it is there
the two of us meet
to renew our mutual
fantasy

Most often 'tis only we
you and me,
as we wrestle in the heat
basted by love's juices
complete

Then overwhelming desires
to share and fulfill each other
gently enters peripherally
A word, a wink, a nod,
an understood mutuality
Together
each surrenders
Attempts one, to the other to please
once more
yes, more,
than ever before

Stoking excitement's flame
the continued thrill of infatuation
alive and burning
fanned by lust,
on the embers of commitment
and total trust

Gently and openly
sharing vulnerabilities
and secrets for one another

Risking to take love
higher and higher
Testing the limits of our desires

Sharing wholly
individual thoughts and fantasies
Learning where they cross and meet
coming together,
as do we

Strange Trim

The sole experience
as good as the first
is a new first again
each time with strange trim
No matter the declination
upon a preconceived numerical scale
nor one's final wink and nod
as one walks out the door,
the in-between spell is rapturous bliss
as tongues and hands rove and roll
over beguiling lips and tips

The titillating excitement
of a first kiss and touch
coupled with infatuation's nervous lust,
the fear of discovery
yet turned away
as excited body parts
over corpus delicti do play

Each new strange encounter
holds its own uniqueness at bay
until it's been ravaged
all night, all day
then familiarity rears its predictable head
as strange becomes commonplace
with her, with him,
and it's time to move on
to tap new strange trim

Strutters

She's got the look
She's dressed to kill
Her eyes say 'E Ticket'
then ask rhetorically, while sliding aside
Interested?
Wanna ride?

Her walk says thrill
Her glare says chill
Her perpetual come-on screams
"I will"
but her attitude informs;
no limitless credit cards
then my friend
you can count on nil

Believing she's ideal,
surreal
Long term possibilities
we don't consider
It's an enviable trophy
and eye-candy piece on our arms
with imagined head pleasures
causing us to jitter

All flash
no substance,
most men don't care
Women point out unabashedly
"one can't have it all,
if there's nothing there"

Plastic procedures
falsifications galore
some double digit
if we're keeping score

Man says "I see
and know it to be
but none of that matters
or bothers me
As long as I can
fawn my Madonna
and later, fondle my whore"

"Does she do the nasty?"
"They all do, eventually"
Only one question remains;
what her price will be?

What will it cost you
to have lust, sex and love
with vamps and vixens
Those self-indulged vultures
posing as doves

your future
your potential
your self-respect
your good name,
your position
your power
your play in the game

your reputation
your new wife
your future wife
your home
your family. . .
your life?

What will it cost you
to stroke her ego daily
Insuring she never tires
leaving you full of doubt
and self-flagellatingly crazy

We asked our expert
about those faux beauties
who are always
struttin',
showin'
hot airin'
and attitude blowin'

"Trust me" he said,
a twinkle in his eye
"There is one thing
none can escape
No matter who they be
nor what may be tried,
or how many times
they attempt to expense it"

"For each and every
Virtually all inevitably
and hence undeniably,
the years and gravity
will override surgical propensities"

"Why jump through hoops
and beat yourself up
to be with one
whose first and only
interest in life
is in the mirror
on the wall,
overwhelmed by insecure attempts
to be the fairest of all"

"I've known a 'Cosmo' or two
a number of pros and back street hookers
Some with money
Others poor as church mice"

"But of the lot
those without the runway ego's
are always nice
and deliciously hot"

He continued explaining
"If I had my choice
who would it be?
The plain and everyday Jane's
or all those others
trapped in their own hype?"

"Why waste your good time
energies and efforts
Why waste your life
on saccharin and plastic,
when those mature and secure
are always fantastic"

Teen Show and Tell

She's struttin' sway back
and standing tall
Protruding pretentious points
leading her way
Postured intentions
producing male enticements
with erectile risings

Small firm breasts
Supple young teats
Pert
Perky
Arresting

Showing expanses of
bronzed terra cotta
soft porcelain skin
Desperate for man's
wanton desires
to handle
stroke
and fondle them

Directed at man's muted
lust filled genital mustering
Her power, the pain
of Blue Balls busting

Staring straight ahead
searching for admirers without moving her head,
her seeking eyes in unison click
while moving theirs and the pulsating tips
of their hardening pricks

Cautiously hoping
Tentative prayer
One might like to lick
and insert his bulging bulbous heat
deep,
inside her wet, sticky
candied sweets

Movements by long practiced design
Her seductive slither
A look of come-hither
Created solely
for a cum-all-over-me appeal
Teasing each mentally
to cop a feel

Virginity intact
she struts away
sway back

The Difference

the difference between
"I love you"
and
"I love fucking you"
;
Nuzzling against the hollow of your sternum
before or after

The opportunity I take
to lick your post ejaculatory drip

Wondering if you will call

Rolling over in the morning
finding you still lying next to me

Hearing a song on the radio
and you proclaiming it as "ours"

Continuing to wish and hope
in response to my friends' advise

Allowing me to suggest your wardrobe
without getting 'that look'

The prospect of having to go out there,
Alone
Again

Saying "I love you"
without feeling guilty

Reaching climax
without fearing you will call out
another's name

Being deep inside of me,
and you are tender
not abusive

Holding my hand in public
instead of walking steadfastly ahead

Ignoring me whenever I speak of
a future with you

The number of times I say
I love you,
to your silence

The Traveler

I once saw an image
of Buddha
in Buda,
Texas
on a trip to see
one of my exes.
Then on a journey
to Wichita Kansas
I met a girl
from Port Aransas
Said she was trying
to get back home
but that she was actually
from Nome,
Alaska.
We traveled together
as far as Reno
where we met a lady
who liked to play Keno
The first one left
the second one stayed
and for about a week we played,
Black Jack.
I won a little
but soon lost my shirt
then met a woman
who liked to flirt,
a lot.
She asked me to join
her and her friend
and so we began
to party hardy

with a case of rum
labeled Bacardi
until I awoke,
and found myself in Denver
no joke, Colorado.
Next off to Aspen
to get some skiing in
it's there I met
a great new friend,
She was a killer,
No, really,
She was on the lamb
wanted for a murder
in Birmingham,
Alabama
down south,
and could she ever use her mouth
Trash talker, you understand
even so she could also use her hand,
for hitch hiking.
We hit it off right away
said I was the first guy she'd met
along the way
who wasn't gay,
We licked
and frolicked
all night one day
then decided to part and separate
guess it was always our predestined fate.
She went West
and I went North,
Dakota

Then caught a ride to Minnesota,
Ya!
Learned they have 10,000 lakes
each with resident mosquitoes
make no mistake,
I became a feast
for a couple of weeks.
Decided to get
'on the road again'
as Willie Nelson
would say,
Hitchhiked all the way
to Florida
on the I-75 freeway corridor.
Landed in West Palm
with a new pair of shades on
Looking the part
met an Aussie bartender
who liked to play darts.
She was a knockout
that was for sure
and oooooooooooh,
how she could purr,
like a raw V8
motor, you know
for days and nights
man could she go
Revved me up
and round
and round,
rubbed my little nub
right into the ground,

I recovered, eventually
but by then she was gone
Maybe back to the land of Oz
I wondered.
Cared not, for South Florida much
So went all the way to the home of the Dutch
Amsterdam you see,
from the states I wanted to flee.
So now I'm traveling by train
on my way to southern Spain,
Iberian Peninsula.
Think I'll stop there
to spend more time
drink some sangria
with a floating lime,
in the glass.
The Spaniards are nice people
so I've heard
an easy place to live
free as a bird
Have chosen either Barcelona,
Malaga
or perhaps Marbella
Understand rich ladies are there
who like to cavort
on the Playa,
del Sol.
One way or the other
believe I'll stop in
to visit my mother,
She lives there,
in Spain that is.

XXX

Cyber sex is my life
It's even better
than doing my wife

All designed
for my release
It's better than living
in ancient Greece

Anything goes
on my computer screen
The women even smile
as I make them scream

Most sites
want to charge a fee
but I searched and searched
and found one that was free

Of course there's no hard core
except for the teasers
They've convinced me all women
are just male pleasers

There's bondage, domination
lots of S & M
On top
On bottom
Her with her
and him with him
Their carnal knowledge
makes my heart and heads spin

The mind is a wonderfully curious thing
it makes me forget about the ring
The one on my finger
which once meant so much
Now I revel
in more and more smut

I'm really okay
I'm not at all ill
I take lots of pills
and watch Dr. Phil

And Oprah
MoPo
Rikki
Montel,
and just for fun
Springer, late night
what the hell

Sure,
I've put some distance
between me and my family
But it's an I
Me
My world
and I live it happily

I just stop in to see
all my favorite XXX's
That's where my mind and body
meet at their nexus

My family waits
for me to come round
To be husband and father
brother and son
But I'd rather have
my cyber fun

Remember,
"it's all about me"
I even bought the T-shirt
for all to see

I'd rather have it my way
and continue to whine
Than admit I could kick
this lifestyle habit
of mine

I'm not responsible
for all I do,
I don't even
have a clue
I'm the victim here,
Don't you see that?
I've exchanged all values
for a cyber trap

So when I am old
lonely
and put away
I can look back,
back on the days

Days I spent drowning
in cyber sex, sex, sex, sex
And blame someone else
for my ruined life's hex . . .

For to stop all this cybering
and avoid it's snare
I would have to not hit
the keyboard keys,
that take me there

You Tube

Like souvenirs taken
from a serial killer's victims
I keep track
of those conquered,
they who've had me

Categorizing by orifices penetrated
showering accolades perpetuated in points
as if awarded by insider trades
or East German judges
Elevated incrementally
as a rising phallus pushes north
by performances given, received

Filming for posterity,
entertainment,
Internet playback stares
Home movies
of those willing to enter
the sadist's lair

No need to attach your name
all known to you will recognize
your sweat soaked brow
face and cleavage heat
Your glistening rump gyrating
to a rhythmic beat
as your sphincter rim is
exposed
explored
exploited

up close, personal
for ogling eyed irises
and masturbatory palms
or hooded button caressing fingertips

a star is born

Branch Isole is the author of nineteen books. Born in Osaka Japan, Branch Isole traveled extensively growing up calling many places home. Finishing high school in Rolling Hills, California he went on to graduate from Texas State University San Marcos, attended graduate school at the University of Houston and received an M.A. Theology degree from Trinity Bible College and Seminary, Newburgh Indiana.

Branch Isole's catalogue of work includes books, eBooks, greeting cards, inspirational gift mats, available at:

www.branchisole.com
www.manaopublishing.com

Other books by Branch Isole
Erotica Series

Seduction ©
Pleasing Women Sexually
ISBN 978-0982658598
eBook ISBN 978-0983574583

Poetic Prose Series

Epigram ©
long story short
ISBN 978-0982658574
eBook ISBN 978-0983574576

Heartstrings of Illusion ©
Distractions and Deceit in Poetic Prose
ISBN 978-0982658543
eBook ISBN 978-0983574545

Dreams and Schemes ©
Tales and Tattles in Poetic Prose
ISBN 978-0982658550
eBook ISBN 978-0983574552

In The Margins ©
where truth lies
ISBN 978-0982658536
eBook ISBN 978-0983574538

Eclectic Electricity ©
unknown poet's parade
ISBN 978-0982658512
eBook ISBN 978-0983574521

Turn Of A Phrase ©
Pivotal Positions in Poetic Prose
ISBN 978-0982658505
eBook ISBN 978-0983574514

Saccharin and Plastic Band Aids ©
Comments in Poetic Prose
ISBN 978-0974769288
eBook ISBN 978-0983574453

Messages In A Bottle ©
Inspirations in Poetic Prose
ISBN 978-0974769295
eBook ISBN 978-0983574446

Reflections On Chrome ©
Parking Lot Confessions in Poetic Prose
ISBN 978-0974769257
eBook ISBN 978-0983574422

Postcards from the Line of Demarcation ©
Points of Separation in Poetic Prose
ISBN 978-0974769264
eBook ISBN 978-0983574439

Seeds of Mana'o ©
Thoughts, Ideas and Opinions in Poetic Prose
ISBN 978-0974769219
eBook ISBN 978-0983574415

Barking Geckos ©
Stories and Observations in Poetic Prose
ISBN 978-0974769226
eBook ISBN 978-0983574408

Spiritual Christianity Series

Even Christians Stumble and Fall ©
Musings of a Struggling Believer
ISBN 978-0974769240
eBook ISBN 978-0983574491

Crucibles ©
Refinement of the Neophyte Christian
ISBN 978-0974769233
eBook ISBN 978-0983574484

Power of Praise ©
Poetry of Spiritual Christianity ™
ISBN 978-0974769271
eBook ISBN 978-0983574477

GOD. . . i believe ©
Simple Steps on the Path
of Spiritual Christianity ™
ISBN 978-0974769202
eBook ISBN 978-0983574460

<u>Self Help Series</u>

Seduction ©
Pleasing Women Sexually
ISBN 978-0982658598
eBook ISBN 978-0983574583

Pathways to Publishing ©
Self-Publishing
Manuscript to Publication
ISBN 978-0982658567
eBook ISBN 978-0983574507

GOD. . . i believe ©
Simple Steps on the Path
of Spiritual Christianity ™
ISBN 978-0974769202
eBook ISBN 978-0983574460